ARACHNOPHOBIA?

How to Avoid Brown Recluse Spider Bites

By Tom Martincic

Dedicated to my faithful wife, Kelly.

Table of Contents

Preface

Brown recluse spiders are one of the most unique spider species on earth. They have six eyes whereas most other spiders have eight.

They don't spin webs to catch prey like many spiders. Their webs are used for making egg sacs but appear to have no other function. Their mobility and thin legs enable them to escape the effects of residual pesticides.

They are scavengers that prefer dead prey 81 percent of the time, and they can eat an insect killed by a pesticide just 24 hours prior. They'll even feed on insects that have been dead for months.

They can easily shift from a 20°F area to a 130° F attic in one day. They can also live for months without food or water.

They are, as one researcher put it, "built for battle." Yet, at the same time they often lose "street fights" to spiders much smaller and weaker than they.

Brown recluse spiderlings have a very high survival rate, and the adult brown recluses survive cold winters by lowering their metabolism to an unbelievable rate. One researcher says that survival is the brown recluse spider's "claim to fame," and that they are the "Green Berets of the spider world" when it comes to survival.

The fact that brown recluses are so unique affects all of us. They are one of the few spiders able to cause us great pain, limb loss or even end our life with one bite.

For this reason, brown recluse spiders, and spiders in general, tend to cause a great amount of fear in the hearts of many.

Brown recluse spiders are commonly mistaken for other spiders that have a more intimidating appearance.

As the owner of a company that specializes in combating brown recluse spiders, numerous photos of wolf spiders and woodlouse spiders are commonly emailed to me, with users seeking the answer to the fearful and sometimes even tearful question, "Could you tell me if this spider is a brown recluse?"

Thankfully, most spider photos sent to me are not the brown recluse spider at all. But knowing the kind of damage one can inflict is enough to cause people to "just make sure." I commonly get emails from those who live outside this dangerous spider's known range, simply because they saw a very scary spider that had some brown in it.

With this book, I hope to help equip you to learn how to identify the spider yourself. While some experts claim that you cannot positively identify one without magnification to count the number of eyes, my own personal experience is that most anyone can identify a recluse species if they know what to look for and are very careful to follow the instructions I provide in this book. At the very least, you will be able to eliminate dozens of species that are commonly mistaken for the dreaded brown recluse.

If you happen to find a brown recluse spider in your home, I will also teach you the steps to take to control an infestation. Brown recluses are notoriously difficult to eliminate once an infestation has developed. In fact, pest control companies will not guarantee that they can eradicate the spider. If you find one that does, they are probably not being honest. Brown recluses commonly breed inside your walls where pesticides cannot reach.

My own personal experience with the spider began when my family and I moved to Missouri in 1999. I woke up in the morning, put on my sweat pants, and sat down at my computer. Soon, I felt a little tickle on the top of my thigh. It was one of those tickles where you aren't sure whether it's an itch or some kind of insect caught inside your clothes. Rather than scratch it, I decided to feel around to see if there might be a lump inside.

Sure enough, there was a little lump between my pants and thigh. I immediately stood up and pulled my sweats back to look inside. I found a brown spider. I gently lowered and stepped out of my sweat pants, and then began to research what kind of spider it might be. Sure enough, it was the brown recluse. Thankfully and surprisingly, it didn't bite me at all. It had crawled into my sweat pants, which were lying on the floor next to my bed during the night. I soon learned that putting articles of clothing on the floor is a really bad idea as this only invites the spiders to "recluse" themselves inside.

My second experience with the brown recluse did result in a bite. We moved to another location in Missouri, and my wife woke up one morning with a brown recluse bite on her arm. She apparently had inadvertently rolled over on the spider while it was crawling on our bed at night. The bite wound got progressively worse until we applied a paste of activated carbon and lobelia tincture to the wound. It completely reversed course and healed up pretty nicely as we continued to apply the paste. Five years later we created a start-up company to offer the powder and herbs together as a Brown Recluse First Aid Kit.

Over the last eight years of talking to customers and researching the behavioral characteristics of this spider, I have found that misinformation is remarkably widespread, even on medical web sites. Nevertheless, even "experts" don't agree on everything, and there is still a lot about the brown recluse spider that we don't know.

However, one thing we do know for sure is that brown recluses are here to stay. The spider actually benefits from growth in human populations because homes are simply an ideal habitat for them to live within. There are ways of preventing bite wounds, but we need to get educated.

Educating you is the purpose of this book.

Chapter 1

Brown Recluse
Behavior and You

This chapter was written so that you may be acquainted with the behavior of the spider. If brown recluse spiders are in your home, being aware of their habits and how most people are bitten can help you avoid becoming a victim.

Brown recluse spiders are so named because they are, by nature, "reclusive." They rarely come out during the day and prefer to do their dirty work (hunting) at night. For this reason, populations of these spiders often go unnoticed.

If they happen to come out during the day, it is likely because something has disturbed them, a male is on the trail of a female, or they haven't had a meal in a while.

The vast majority of brown recluse spider bites are from male spiders. Males spend most of their time roaming around, hunting for prey and females.

Males are more likely to be encountered and more likely to bite when disturbed. Females are calmer and must be provoked severely to bite.

If you set spider traps in your home, on average about one out of four specimens will be female.

Females tend to stay in one general place, producing offspring in their egg sacs (described later).

It is their reclusiveness, along with the night hunting, that causes such problems for us—yet also causes them to be so successful in freely breeding inside our homes. They have a preference for dry conditions in the wild, where they are typically found under rocks, especially around bluffs, and under bark or inside logs.

In homes that do have brown recluses, they were found outside the home in every instance.

Homes are ideal because they are dry and there are food sources throughout. But in homes they often go unnoticed until the day you happen upon them unexpectedly.

Newer homes are just as likely to contain infestations as older ones. Larger homes had a slightly larger number of brown recluses, but the difference was not statistically significant.

If you leave clothing on the floor before going to bed, the spider might see it as a suitable place to hide out during the day. You then put the clothing on with the spider snuggled inside for a good day's sleep. But getting squashed between your skin and clothing is scary. He really didn't set out to hurt you; he is just biting in self-defense.

The reclusive nature might also cause him to hide out in your dresser drawers, the children's toy box, behind picture frames, under furniture, inside your laundry basket or hamper, the clothing rack in your closet, inside your shoes, or inside boxes or totes. He also might find good hiding places in your garage, shed, wood piles, closets and any undisturbed clutter. If the place is normally undisturbed, the spider is far more likely to be found.

Clutter alone does not necessarily increase the number of brown recluses you will find in a house, but clutter certainly will increase the number of places where they are able to hide.

This can be detrimental if you are using pesticides to try and eradicate the spider. After treatments, the spiders are unharmed and unaffected because they are in the clutter. Thus, they are free to roam about your house and take advantage of all the dead prey (see below).

The fact that they hunt at night poses another problem. They can crawl up the dust ruffles of your bed and roam around, looking for food while you sleep. According to researchers, most victims are bitten while they are sleeping.

They are also known for falling off ceilings. In our Missouri home, I've seen them do this. If you have any kind of significant infestation, dead brown recluses will often be seen inside ceiling mounted light fixtures. Since they move in and out of walls and ceilings, the light fixture is a potential entry and exit point.

Unlike many spiders, brown recluses do not spin webs to find their food. They prefer instead to hunt. They roam around the house looking for insects to eat and partners with which to breed.

Whether the insect is dead or alive doesn't really matter. In fact, lab experiments show that after testing 147 spiders by offering them a choice between identical prey items (one dead and one alive), the brown recluse spider preferred the dead prey 81.4 percent of the time. This is a finding never before witnessed in any other spider. The brown recluse spider is truly unique!

But why does the spider prefer dead insects over living ones? The reason is not known with 100 percent certainty, but one possibility is that brown recluses, in spite of their incredible ability to survive and adapt, are somewhat fragile and lose limbs relatively easily.

Brown recluse spiders will often lose street fights to organisms that we don't consider deadly at all including ants, beetles, other spiders and even insects they regard as prey (like grasshoppers and crickets).

Sometimes a brown recluse will even lay motionless and let potential prey walk all over it rather than risk injury by attacking. They will even run away from them at times!

In the laboratory, researchers were trying to feed yellow mealworm larvae to brown recluses, but they ran into a problem with the mealworms eating the spiders. So they began killing the mealworms prior to putting them in the enclosures with the spiders, and the spiders readily ate them.

Their preference for dead insects make homes a place where they can maintain large populations because these locations often have far more dead insects than living ones. This also helps them get through the winters. Brown recluses can be active year-round, but do have increased activity in warmer months.

Insects are attracted to homes for various reasons, but often will die once they are inside due to injury, lack of food and water, or pesticides. But a brown recluse only needs one insect every couple of months or so to survive. Thus, houses can easily support a large brown recluse population.

One home can support anywhere from 50 to several thousand brown recluses. If you happen to find one, it is unlikely that it is alone, and it is highly likely that there are a lot more. In field studies, the average home with an existing infestation had 60 to 80 brown recluses.

One family in Kansas had an infestation of some 2000 of these spiders. Remarkably, no one in the family had been bitten. This isn't necessarily unusual, but almost everyone in their indigenous areas knows of someone who has been bitten by a brown recluse.

So what kind of insects do brown recluse spiders prefer to eat? Seeking the answer to this question, Kansas University researchers conducted experiments a few years ago to determine the spiders' preferences. Based on their research, brown recluse spiders consistently chose larger prey in choice tests. The results were as follows:

1 - Grasshoppers
2 – Waxmoths
3 – Crickets
4 – Honeybees
5 – Cockroaches
6 – Houseflies
7 - House spiders
8 – Pillbugs
9 – Termites
10 – Ladybugs

Small prey, or prey with mechanical barriers or defensive chemicals, were consistently avoided or even ignored.

The spider's attack strategy consists of a sudden lunge and then a bite, usually on the prey's appendages such as legs or antennae. The spider may touch the prey with its palps before delivering a first bite.

If the prey is particularly mobile, such as a housefly or ladybug, the spider will keep a grip on it until the venom takes effect. If the prey is adept at fighting, in just a fraction of a second it will bite and then step back to observe from a distance until the prey is overcome by the venom.

Multiple bites are common with further attacks occurring on more central attachments or the main body. Then it will move in to feed. It may spin its silk to further immobilize the prey.

But the brown recluse isn't impervious to trouble. The spider can also easily become prey.

The cobweb weeaving spiders (*A. tepidariorum* and *S. triangulosa*) often seen in homes are the main predators of the brown receluse. More information on this is provided in chapter five.

Recluse spiders have a remarkable tolerance for heat. Studies show that they are able to withstand temperatures up to 161 F! Basically, they are built for hot climates, and this is the reason they are most common in the mid to southern section of the United States.

However, they are also capable of lowering their metabolism to a very remarkable rate to survive a very cold winter with sub-zero temperatures.

Brown recluse spiders have a strong dislike for drafty places like doorways and windows. They also hate vibrations, so areas where vibration is constant will deter them. However, they don't seem to mind areas of low frequency vibration like the furnace and water heater.

In fact, the furnace and water heater area is a very common location for brown recluse spiders and insects. The condensation provides an oasis in an otherwise dry indoors, and brown recluses tend to hang out and grab regular meals from wayfaring insects looking for a drink.

Brown recluses themselves though can live a remarkably long time without food or water. The ability to survive dry and barren conditions is one of the most amazing attributes of this unique spider.

The next picture is a male brown recluse spider that was placed in an airtight container about 2-inches in height, approximately the size of a doorknob.

After having its last meal, this lonely brown recluse spider lived in the container for five and a half months off that meal along with the air left inside.

Males are known to have a shorter life than females. One must wonder how long a female can live without food, water and air.

Males are more likely to be seen roaming around your home than females. Females tend to stay near their nest. They will typically find a place to breed in an undisturbed location, such as inside a box or inside your walls. The fact that they often breed behind drywall is what makes these spiders so difficult to eradicate. Pesticides simply cannot be sprayed there.

The males are much more mobile, and if pesticides happen to be sprayed, they can simply flee.

Once a pesticide has dried, however, they don't have a significant residual effect on brown recluses.

Actually, in some ways pesticides can be beneficial to the brown recluse because the pesticides kill web-spinning spiders that would otherwise prey on them, and all the insects killed by the pesticide provide easier and more plentiful meal opportunities. Brown recluses can eat an insect killed by pesticides just 24 hours prior and suffer no harm.

However, pesticides may irritate or damage the nervous system of the spider, causing them to be more aggressive than normal.

If a pesticide were to be sprayed directly on the spider, it probably would die. But then again, it would probably also die if you sprayed water all over it.

The brown recluse is truly an unusual creature!

Breeding

Eighty percent of reproduction occurs in May, June or July but may occur as early as February.

With fine sensory hairs covering his body along with the sense of touch, a male can track a female by a scent she leaves on surfaces she has walked on.

The male must announce himself by performing certain maneuvers or courtship dances to lure the female. If he does not, she may consider him to be suitable prey. The maneuvers include moving his palpi or legs, and if successful, she will submit to his advances and mating will ensue. Usually, they separate in peace.

The male may mate again with the same female or with another female.

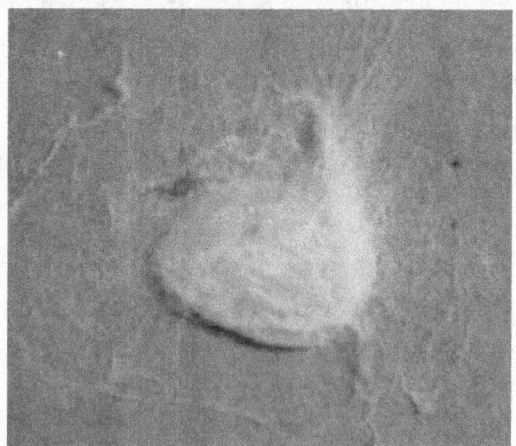

Recluse Nest with Juvenile Spiderling Nearby.

She will deposit her eggs in off-white silk cases measuring about 1/3-inch to 2/3-inch in diameter. She then carries them to a suitable, safe place.

Contrary to popular myth, the females do not lay eggs in a person's ear canal.

They may place the egg sac near the stem of a plant, or if living in a home, they will place it in a box or other out of the way location. If you find an egg sac with irregular webbing all around it, it may indeed be a brown recluse egg sac. Look around for the presence of a female brown recluse nearby.

An egg sac has an average of about 40 to 50 eggs, and females typically choose to make more than one egg sac during a breeding season. One female may make 300 eggs in her lifetime.

Egg sacs have a hatch rate of 40 to 80 percent, and females will require more than one mating over their lifetimes to remain fertile. As they age, the egg production and survivability of their offspring appears to decline.

After setting up her nest, young spiders will emerge in three to six weeks, and they will stay with their mother until the third or fourth molt before dispersing. Full maturity will be reached after the eighth molt, as long as food and temperatures are adequate. The survival rate is remarkably high.

Their prolific breeding ability in stealth locations is a major reason why they are so difficult to eradicate. Of course, this is to our detriment.

After dispersing from the nest, young brown recluses may establish home territories, where they will stay for additional molts. Brown recluses are active in temperatures ranging from 45 F to 110 F, but bites can occur at any time of the year in a heated home where there is a constant temperature.

In fact, brown recluse populations can increase in your home during the winter because of the warmth compared to the outside air. Normally, the spider will simply enter a state of homeostasis until the warmer weather comes. But if the spider is in your home, there is less of a need for it.

For this reason, homeowners will continue to see brown recluse spiders during the winter. We've personally seen them in our dresser drawers and roaming around the house in the middle of January.

If they are having trouble finding any food in the house, they may go into a state of homeostasis right in our dresser drawers, closets, boxes, or wherever they think they are safe.

We don't see them quite as frequently in the winter, but they are here nonetheless. We intentionally allow them to live with us so that we can study them. We are no longer afraid of them because we are confident in the treatment we use.

Brown recluse life cycles are between one and four years, but in laboratory conditions they have lived as long as seven years.

Chapter 2

Brown Recluse
Anatomy and You

The brown recluse is part of the *Loxosceles* genus of spiders. *Loxosceles* is a Latin translation of a combination of Greek words meaning something like "slanted leg." As part of the *Sicariidae* family, its cousin, the long living assassin spider in the southern hemisphere, can also deliver a venomous bite.

Adult brown recluse spiders are yellowish-tan to dark brown. They have long, thin gray to dark brown legs covered with very short, dark hairs. The hairs are nearly invisible from a distance, and they give the abdomen a slightly fuzzy appearance.

The picture below shows an adult brown recluse. A full page, high resolution photo is supplied in the photos section of this book.

Both male and female spiders are similar in appearance and are equally venomous.

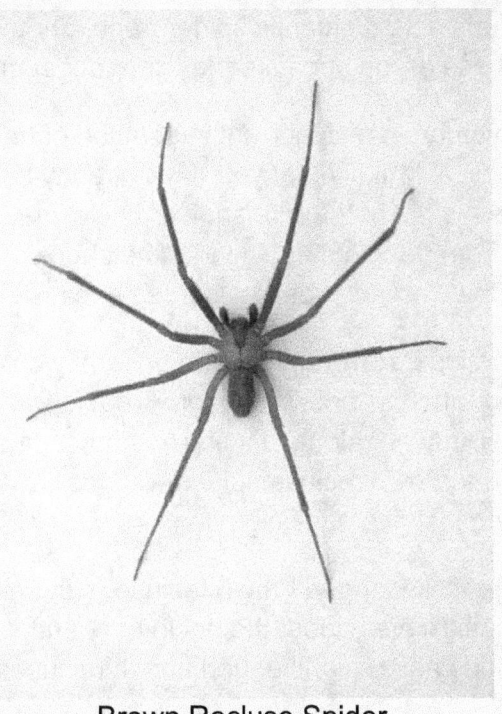

Brown Recluse Spider

The Legs and Feet

Brown recluses do not have "sticky" feet like other spiders or insects. They have tiny pinchers or claws at the end of their legs, which grab surfaces as they walk. For this reason, brown recluses are usually (but not always) found on the ground rather than climbing up walls and across ceilings. If they are walking across a drywall ceiling or wall, they are usually moving very slow, being careful to find some kind of rough surface to grasp before proceeding.

Rougher textures with nooks and crannies will give them more mobility, but very smooth surfaces like sinks and bathtubs act as gigantic spider traps. They often get stuck in these areas because they cannot get out.

If you have a significant infestation of brown recluse spiders, it is very likely that you have already come across one inside a sink, bathtub or shower enclosure. Bites have occurred from people stepping into the shower without looking. One woman even lost her leg because of it.

The legs are long, thin and uniformly colored. If it loses a leg, another one will not grow back. However, the spider will likely get along just fine without it. In a laboratory, a brown recluse spider lived for several months after having lost five of its eight legs.

The three legged brown recluse (pictured below) feeds, hunts, moves about the enclosure, and is every bit as venomous as an eight legged brown recluse:

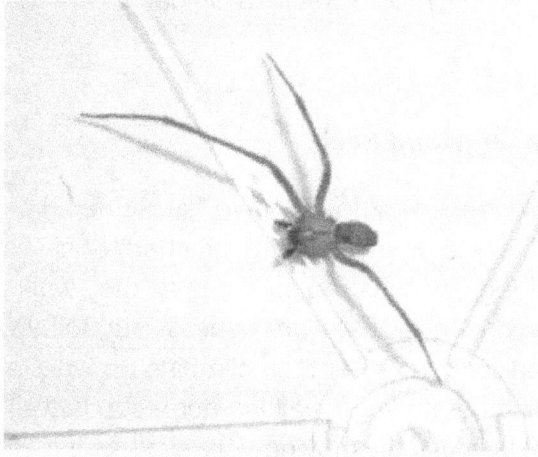

Three Legged Brown Recluse

Interestingly, a brown recluse can still bite for up to eight minutes after removing all eight legs **and the**

abdomen! This means even if there is only a head left, it can still deliver a nasty bite.

The Fangs

The fangs of a brown recluse spider are unusually strong. The strong fangs are very helpful to the spider when it comes to piercing through the strong exoskeletons of beetles and other prey, but the strength of the fangs is also the reason why brown recluse spiders are able to pierce human skin.

But in spite of how strong the fangs are, they are tinier than you might think. Unlike snakes, which can inject venom deep into human skin, the spider's smaller size means that most of the venom is injected near the skin's surface.

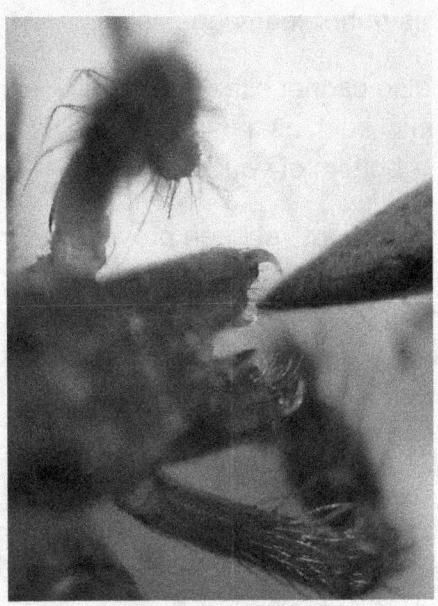

Brown Recluse Fangs

The above photo, taken by Kansas University researchers, is a high macro shot showing the spider trying to bite the end of a regular no. 10 staple. Notice that the fangs aren't even as long as the staple is thick.

They are too short to bite through most fabrics so they likely need bare skin in order to successfully injure you. In every verified case of a brown recluse bite, the spider was directly against the skin of the victim.

In a lab it was shown that brown recluses will not attempt to bite if something touches their legs, their underside or anywhere on their body unless there is pressure. Pressure meaning they feel like they are getting squashed by something, such as getting caught inside clothes, shoes, or being rolled on while crawling on your bed at night.

Almost all brown recluse bites are from incidental contact like this rather than aggression.

They also cannot bite through thick epidermal layers of the skin such as those found in the palm of your hand or on the bottom of your foot.

While it has not yet been proven, it is believed by some that it may not be possible for the spider to just come up and bite a person without some kind of back pressure to force the spider against the skin.

The Size of Brown Recluses

As the photo below shows, brown recluses vary in size, with the average size of the spider being a little larger than the size of a quarter.

But what is the largest ever recorded?

Of 86,000 spiders collected and reviewed by the Recluse Community Project at Kansas University, the largest recorded brown recluse spider was a male specimen measuring 2.874 inches from the end of one leg to the other, which is about the size of three quarters, end to end, and larger than the width of an average sized computer mouse.

The Violin Marking

The most distinguishing characteristic in the brown recluse's appearance is the presence of a violin shaped marking on its back.

Violin Enhanced Photo

The above picture is edited to highlight the violin/fiddle shape on the spider's back, also called the cephalothorax.

The presence of a violin-like marking on the back of a spider is not conclusive evidence of a brown recluse. There are other species of spiders which have markings that resemble violins or banjos (see chapter six).

Because of this marking, the brown recluse is sometimes called the "violin spider" or "fiddleback spider."

The legs of brown recluse spiders are long and thin. They may have a silky appearance due to the fine, almost invisible hairs covering them. They are a solid color and never have bands of colors or stripes on any of them.

The lack of stripes and bands on a brown recluse's legs is an important part of identification. Brown recluse spiders do not have any significant pigment variations on their abdomen.

If you see a spider that has any markings on its tail end, it cannot be a brown recluse spider. As the photos show, the color of the abdomen is tan to brown.

Fuller, Lighter Brown Abdomen   Smaller, Dark Brown Abdomen

The difference in color and size of the abdomen will change if the spider has recently eaten. If the spider has recently had a meal, the abdomen will be full looking and may appear lighter in color. If the spider hasn't had a meal in a while, it turns to a darker brown and can get very small. If its abdomen starts to shrivel a little at the end, as seen in the above photo, the spider may be near death if it doesn't get a meal soon.

Notice, however, that this is the only significant difference between the two spiders. Notice that both abdomens have a fairly solid, uniform color.

The Eyes

The most distinguishing characteristic is that brown recluses have only six eyes.

Most spiders have eight eyes, often arranged in two rows, but the brown recluse spider has six eyes arranged in a triangular pattern of three sets (see below picture).

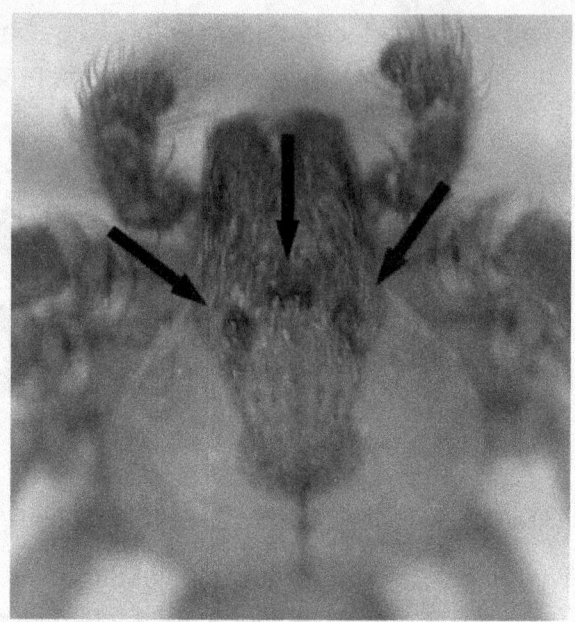
Brown Recluse Eyes

The three sets are called dyads, and if you can see them clearly at the bell end of the violin marking, this is clear proof that the spider is a recluse species.

Juveniles

Juvenile brown recluse spiders are a lighter tan in color, and there may be no recognizable "violin" marking.

Thankfully, they are also unable to bite humans due to the fact that their fangs at this stage are not likely to be large enough to puncture human skin.

The above photo doesn't really show it, but the spiders at this stage are extremely small and hard to notice unless they are grouped together.

Difference Between Male and Female

The differences between a male and female brown recluse can be difficult to determine. A good general rule is that males have longer legs and smaller bodies while females have shorter legs with larger bodies.

However, to determine their sex most accurately, it requires a little bit of knowledge about spider anatomy.

See the below diagram and notice the part of the spider's body called the "pedipalp" or "palp" for short:

Anatomy of the Brown Recluse

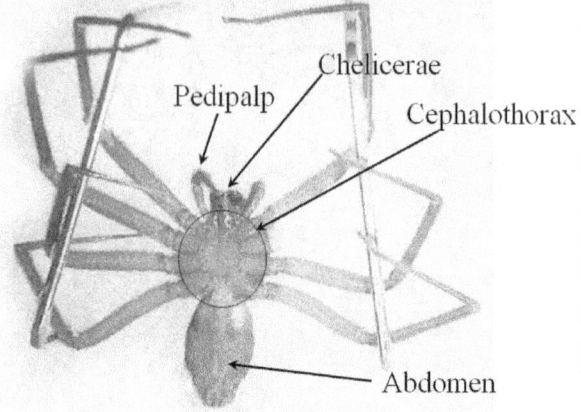

Source: Kansas University

The primary difference between male and female brown recluses is the palp. The female's palp looks more like another leg:

Source: Kansas University

In this picture, notice that the male brown recluse's pedipalp looks less like a leg. This is because it is designed for sperm transfer and has many hard (sclerotized) areas:

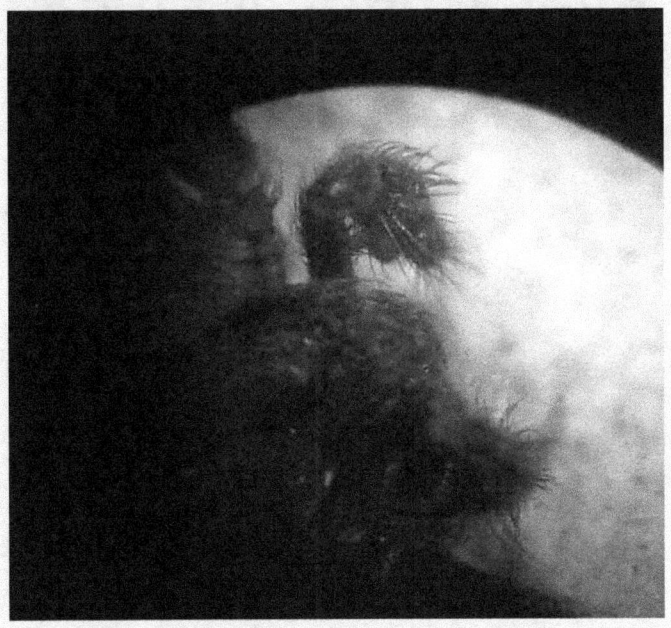

Chapter 3

Just Where are these Spiders Located?

The highest concentrations of brown recluse spiders are found in Kansas, Missouri, Arkansas and Oklahoma. As an example of their abundance, a 75-minute search of a barn in Missouri yielded 40 spiders. One study in Missouri found this spider in 70 percent of the homes that were sampled.

The abundance of the spider in Missouri has resulted in almost every lifelong Missouri resident knowing someone who has personally been bitten by the spider… or has themself been a bite victim.

Due to the mobility of society and this spider's tendency to "recluse" itself in boxes and shipping cartons, it can be found nearly anywhere.

However, established populations are most common in the following states:

- Nebraska

- Iowa

- Illinois

- Indiana

- Ohio

- Kansas

- Oklahoma

- Missouri

- Arkansas

- Kentucky

- Tennessee

- Texas

- Alabama

- Mississippi

- The panhandle of Florida

- Georgia

- North Carolina

- Louisiana

However, the brown recluse spider is just one out of _eleven_ native recluse species living in the United States. The brown recluse is the most common of all, and less is known about the potential for envenomation with the other species, but it is likely to be similar.

For instance, the desert recluse is the second most common recluse species in the United States. One scientist reported that he allowed himself to be bitten by the desert recluse and it produced a necrotic lesion similar to that of the brown recluse.

The other recluse species are:

The Mediterranean Recluse (_Loxosceles rufescens_)

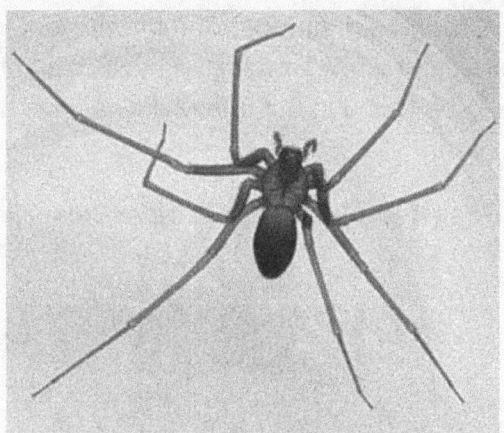

Mediterranean Recluse
Source: Ohio State University

Originating in the Mediterranean region of Europe and Northern Africa, it has been found in Arkansas, Hawaii, Ohio, Florida and in various cities throughout the United States. It looks the same as a brown recluse, except the eyes are spaced slightly different and it has distinctive genitalia. Considered to be equally venomous, this spider might actually be the culprit when a brown recluse spider is blamed—especially if a necrotic bite wound is found on a person living outside the brown recluse spider's common range.

However, the spider's distribution is fairly scattered. When it is found, it seems to prefer crawl spaces, basements and cave-like areas. Populations of these spiders have been found in caves in North America.

The spider is more common in Israel, found throughout buildings and basements. In Israel, Turkey, Australia and Greece, the spider is proven to be responsible for necrotic bite wounds.

In Israel a number of migrant workers were bitten by the spider while working with citrus plants. It is more likely to be found in commercial dwellings than residential.

The Desert Recluse (*Loxosceles deserta*)

Desert Recluse
Source: R. Vetter

The desert recluse is found in the desert southwest in the United States from the eastern half of California to the southern tip of Nevada. It is less likely to live with humans and seems to prefer native vegetation, especially in packrat dens.

The Texas Recluse (*Loxosceles devia*)

Texas Recluse

Similar in appearance to the brown recluse, the marking is duskier and the shape is reduced to a bit more of a "Y" than a violin (See above photo). This spider is found throughout the southern third of Texas and into Mexico. It lives in buildings, under stones and in rodent burrows.

Because it likes to live in buildings, like the brown recluse, this spider should be considered medically significant. Furthermore, since it does not have the pronounced violin pattern on its back, some may choose to dismiss this as a dangerous spider. If you live in south Texas, look for the "Y" pattern on the back of any spiders. Also, as always, look for the three sets of eyes in a semi-circle.

The Chilean Recluse (*Loxosceles laeta*)

Chilean Recluse

This is the most dangerous recluse species of all. It is even more toxic than the brown recluse. Larger than most recluse species, its highly toxic venom will cause death in three to four percent of cases.

It is indigenous to South America, but due to the mobility of society it is hitching rides to all kinds of places and establishing populations. The spider has fully established populations in Los Angeles, California. Infestations have also been found in Vancouver, BC; Cambridge, MA; and in the state of Florida.

They seem to thrive in human dwellings, and like the brown recluse, they can survive long periods of time without food or water.

The Grand Canyon Recluse (*Loxosceles kaiba*)

Found only in the Grand Canyon area, little is known or has been published about this spider.

The Arizona Recluse (*Loxosceles arizonica*)

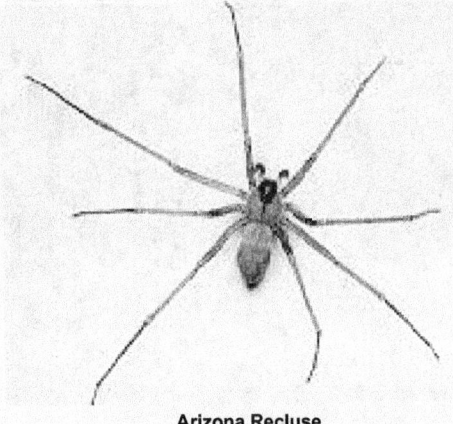

Arizona Recluse
Source: Ohio State University

Found only in Arizona, it is less likely to live with humans than brown recluses. However, envenomations have occurred. The violin pattern on the back is not as pronounced as the brown recluse spider. This species tends to feast on night-active insects such as carpenter ants.

The Martha's Recluse (*Loxosceles Martha*)

Found in southern California, little has been published about this spider.

The Big Bend Recluse (*Loxosceles blanda*)

Found in west Texas, it looks nearly identical to the brown recluse.

The Apache Recluse (*Loxosceles apachea*)

Apache Recluse

Another spider that looks nearly identical to the brown recluse, though the abdomen appears to be a bit darker color.

Russell's Recluse (*Loxosceles russelli*)

This species is found only in Death Valley, California. As with the Grand Canyon recluse, little has been published about this spider.

The Tucson Recluse (*Loxosceles sabina*)

Found in southeast Arizona around the foothills and canyons of the Santa Catalina Mountains, this spider is typically discovered under debris in the dry desert.

The Baja Recluse (*Loxosceles palma*)

Found in southern California to northern Baja, Mexico. As with some of the other less common species, little has been published about this spider.

As you can see, not all recluse species have an identical violin shaped marking, but most of them have a similarly shaped marking on their back. The presence of this, along with the three sets of eyes in a semicircle shape, can be helpful in positively identifying the spider as a *Loxosceles* species of some kind. Each should be considered venomous and dangerous.

The territories where brown recluse spiders are more common may be affected by the recent warm weather trends, which some believe are from global warming or greenhouse gasses affecting weather patterns.

The current warming trend may cause brown recluses to take up residence in areas that are further north than what is considered to be their normal range.

A new study, published in the 3/25/2012 edition of PLoS ONE, suggests that the spider could eventually establish indigenous breeding populations in states like Wisconsin, Michigan, New York and South Dakota.

Can the brown recluse be found outside its normal range? Yes. Due to its preference for boxes, shipping crates and clothing, the brown recluse spider can hitch a ride to most anywhere.

Will they establish a breeding population outside their known range? Not likely, but it would be difficult to use the word "impossible" because homes are such suitable living conditions for the spider. But establishing a growing, breeding population outside their indigenous area would be highly unlikely.

If you live outside its indigenous area, and you happen to see a spider with a violin shaped marking on its back plus three sets of eyes in the semi-circle shape, it may not be a brown recluse, but it could instead be one of the other recluse species. The spider would likely be of interest to local universities.

If you live in the desert southwest, Southern California, or the southern half of Texas, it may be a desert recluse or other kind of recluse listed above.

If you live in other areas of the country, which are outside the known range of the brown recluse spider, you may be looking at a Mediterranean recluse.

If you live in Los Angeles, it is more likely the highly toxic Chilean recluse. Eradication of this spider would be very highly recommended.

Other Kinds of Potentially Venomous Spiders

Another spider, unrelated to the brown recluse, yet believed by some to also cause necrotic bite wounds, is the **hobo spider.**

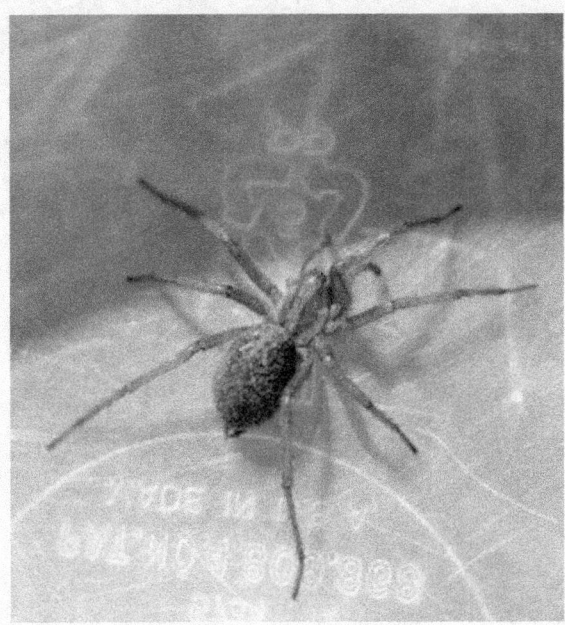
Hobo Spider, Source: Dr. Lee Ostrum

Found throughout the Pacific Northwest, hobo spiders are potentially aggressive. It is believed that their aggression may be due to poor eyesight, and they appear most aggressive when guarding their egg sac.

One study shows that the spider's venom can cause necrosis in rabbits, but then another study is believed by some to have refuted that claim.

The spider has not been specifically proven to cause a necrotic bite wound in humans, but proving a bite wound's origin is notoriously difficult to do. One would have to physically see the spider biting them, and then catch the spider and bring it in for identification, confirmed by an arachnologist.

Whenever a person living in the Pacific Northwest experiences necrosis, a brown recluse spider may be blamed when, in fact, they are not indigenous to that particular area of the country. Perhaps the real culprit is the hobo spider.

Yellow sac spider bites are also believed by some experts to produce necrosis.

Yellow Sac Spider
Courtesy Richard Bartz

Pale yellow in color, the yellow sac spider and related species are found throughout the world, including the United States and parts of Canada. The spider's color may vary depending on the color of its last meal. For instance, if it ate a green caterpillar it may have a greener color to it.

They are about the size of a nickel and there may be a thin stripe going down the center of the abdomen. It is commonly found in homes and buildings, and can spin a funnel shaped web at the edge of your walls and ceilings. If they are disturbed, however, they will typically drop to the floor. The sac is their daytime retreat after spending a night of hunting.

You can inspect your home for these spiders by looking in the upper corners of rooms, behind pictures, or on window moldings, blinds and curtains. Look also for the small, white, paper-like egg sacs and vacuum them up. Be sure to dispose of the bag in a location where they aren't able to re-infest your home.

Yellow sac spider venom is believed to be necrotic, but this has been disputed. If it does produce necrosis, it will not be as severe as a brown recluse bite.

Chapter 4

Bite Photos and Information

Chapter 4 – Bite Photos and Information

Brown recluse spiders are one of the few spiders in the United States that are considered to be medically significant.

Black widow spiders (*Latrodectus*) are the other species, but their venom is completely different than that of a brown recluse.

Black widow venom is a neurotoxin, meaning that it attacks the nervous system. Symptoms of black widow bites would include strong muscle contractions, which can be very painful, similar to what tetanus sufferers experience, especially in the abdomen.

Headaches, tearing, tremors, salivation, nausea and vomiting are secondary symptoms which may accompany the muscle contractions. Due to the invention of antivenin, however, black widow bites are rarely ever fatal.

Brown recluse venom is quite different than that of the black widow. It contains a minimum of eight or nine different enzymes, with the most important one being sphingomyelinase D. Sphingomyelinase D is the most active enzyme in the venom and is thought to be most responsible for tissue destruction. Necrosis, which is the death of living tissue, can be grossly visible in only 24 hours after envenomation.

Mainly around the bite wound area, envenomation causes a decrease of platelets in the blood, alters the clotting time, breaks down red blood cells, and damages the lining of blood vessels. Bites in fatty areas seem to result in the most damage due to the lipase and other components of the venom acting directly on the fatty tissue.

As a result of the venom, the body attacks and splits up red blood cells, a process called hemolysis. A person may feel very fatigued, and their urine may turn dark in color. In severe cases, up to 40 percent of the blood volume can be lost.

Systemic symptoms can also include nausea, a high grade fever up to 105 F, blood abnormalities, nausea, chills and arthritic symptoms. Some victims may experience a loss in blood platelet count. Others may experience a rash similar to that found in scarlet fever, especially those with higher envenomations.

Severe systemic symptoms could include seizures, coma, kidney failure or even death.

When bitten, a burning sensation or pin prick may be felt, but some victims never feel anything. Within six hours the area may begin to itch, along with exhibiting redness due to the increase of blood flow to capillaries of the affected area.

An irregularly shaped ring often will appear around the bite wound due to the changes in blood supply to the area with the highest quantity of venom.

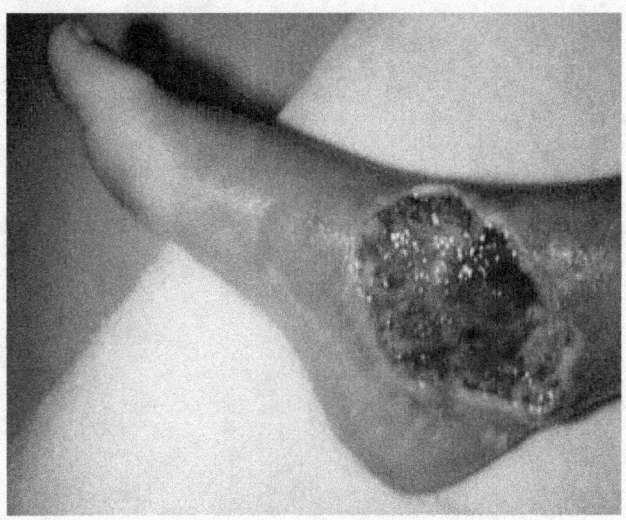

Brown Recluse Bite

The above bite wound occurred to a woman who was taking a shower and noticed the spider on her foot as she was exiting the shower enclosure. She eventually had to have the leg amputated below the knee due to an infection that developed and then progressed until it eventually went into the bone.

The brown recluse is able to control the amount of venom it injects whenever it bites, so some bites may result in only mild discomfort or no pain at all.

Like snakes, brown recluses are also believed to be capable of delivering a "dry bite" containing no venom at all. Spiders that are crushed while trying on clothing or rolled over on a bed at night are most likely to deliver a high quantity of venom.

Brown recluse bites can mimic symptoms of various skin conditions, so finding the spider that bit you is important when seeking to confirm an actual brown recluse bite.

Medical issues and skin conditions that may mimic the symptoms found in brown recluse bites are:

Lyme disease

Cellulitis

Necrotizing fasciitis

Herpes simplex

Pyoderma gangrenosum

Side effects from drugs

Dermatitis

Diabetic or venous stasis ulcers

Ecthyma gangrenosum

MRSA

Polyarteritis nodosa

Sporotrichosis

Tularemia

Chagas' disease

Lymphomatoid papulosis

Boils

Leg or venous ulcers.

Cutaneous/focal vasculitis

For this reason, the medical staff should confirm the bite by examining the spider's number of eyes (six).

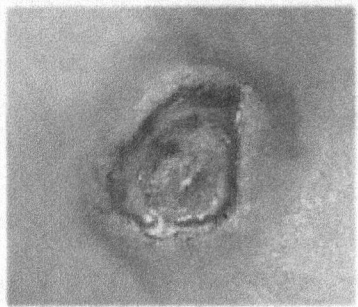

Source: University of Nebraska

Bite wounds with significant envenomation typically progress very quickly, with the localized area turning to a reddish blue color, followed by a blister or bubble in the skin.

The dead skin may slough away within a few days, leaving an open ulcer or crater in the skin.

The open ulcer can take weeks or months to heal, and doctors typically debride and clean the wound periodically while prescribing antibiotics to ward off infection. Significant envenomations my even require skin grafts (see below), or in rare cases, fester for years.

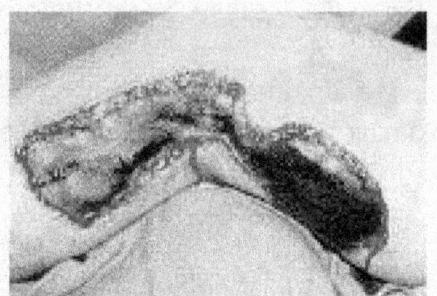

Three Months After Skin Graft
Alabama A & M University

Remarkably, a recluse bite wound can progress to being as large as 12 inches, the size of a dinner plate. These photos were taken 11 days after a brown recluse bite:

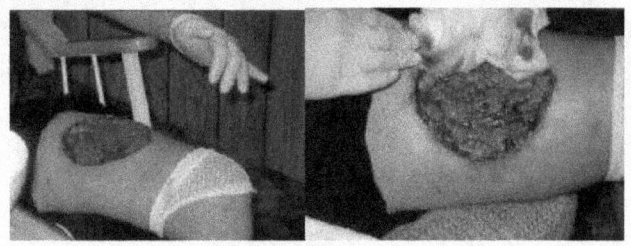

If the bite wound does completely heal, it is possible for it to return again later. It may be prompted by a bruise or return on an annual basis. It might even reappear in a different location, often influenced by gravity. This occurs if the body does not adequately combat or expel the venom. It can occur even if the victim is treated with skin grafts.

The below pictures were sent to us by Cora Rich of Scott County, Tennessee. This bite wound was in its tenth year of recurrence.

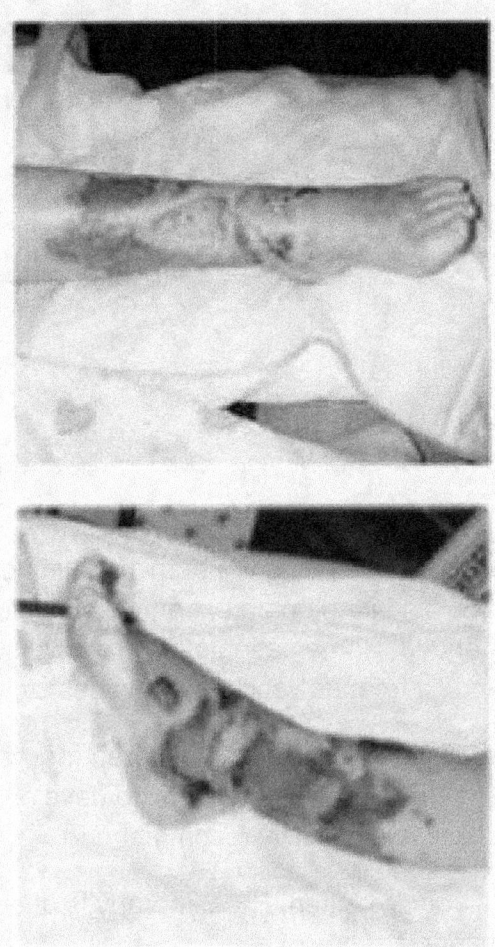

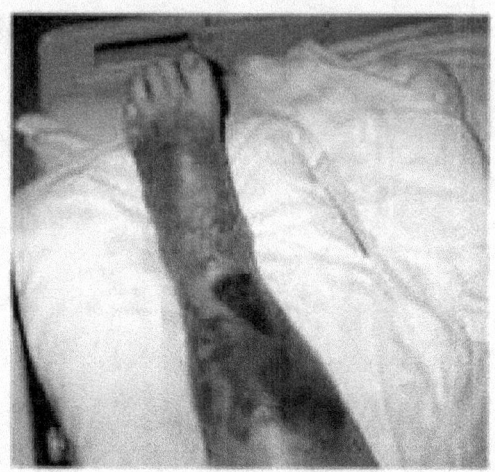

Doctor and hospital treatments vary, with the most common response being the administration of antibiotics. If the victim was bitten on an extremity, elevation is generally recommended. Some patients may receive steroid treatments, a tetanus vaccine or analgesics.

Bite victims are also monitored for systemic symptoms. If systemic symptoms do develop, hospitalization is typically recommended.

If you are bitten, **RICE** therapy is often recommended:

R – Rest is helpful. It may alleviate symptoms such as nausea and headache as the venom spreads beyond the local area.

I – Ice packs help slow the venom's effects and numb the pain.

C – Compression can also help to prevent venom from spreading.

E – Elevation of the affected area can help to reduce pain and swelling.

None of the treatments used in the medical profession are considered to be curative, but are attempts at managing the bite wound and keeping secondary problems at bay.

Secondary complications from brown recluse bites can result in loss of legs, arms, or as in a recent case for a woman in Georgia, the loss of her breast.

Severe systemic complications are most likely to be seen in children less than seven years of age (due to their low body mass in comparison to the quantity of venom), those with compromised immune systems, or the elderly.

However, there are exceptions to this.

For instance, in 2008, 40-year-old Rita Brumm of St. Louis County, Missouri, died at Barnes-Jewish hospital as a result of complications from a spider that bit her as she retrieved a sweater from her closet.

In 2009, a coroner confirmed that 42-year-old Keith Reed of Evansville, Indiana was found dead in his home after a brown recluse spider bit him on the leg while camping. The day prior to his death, Reed had a fever and was in a lot of pain.

However, most deaths occur in young children, such as 5-year-old Nicholas Robinson, who was bitten while playing outside his home about 70 miles south of Nashville, Tennessee. The boy was taken to a doctor who thought he was suffering from a virus rather than a bite. The child was sent home and then was rushed to the hospital that night. He was experiencing hypersalivation, sweating and neurological problems before he died. The state medical examiner confirmed that his death was due to a brown recluse bite.

The symptoms that Nicholas experienced weren't the run-of-the-mill symptoms for brown recluse envenomations, which add to the mystery of what this spider is capable of inflicting on us.

Pain levels vary widely and have been described by victims as non-existent, or second only to childbirth. Pain may become intolerable within 12 to 24 hours, especially if on an arm or a leg.

Deaths are more often from internal systemic symptoms, but not always. Sometimes fatal secondary infections will develop. Severe internal symptoms are more rare than external.

Natural methods of dealing with brown recluse envenomations include the use of plantain or activated carbon poultices.

My own personal experience with the spider has resulted in 100 percent confidence in the use of activated carbon, combined with an herbal solution of plantain, echinacea and lobelia. The liquid solution is combined with the activated carbon powder to a toothpaste-like consistency and applied to the bite wound every one to two hours. As the bite wound heals, the frequency of application is decreased as well.

We began marketing the combination of ingredients as a Brown Recluse First Aid Kit in 2004, and have received raving reviews from customers. The key ingredient, activated carbon, is already used in the medical community to treat food and drug poisoning. Applying it topically to a bite wound is simply an extension of its current use, and it is applied to adsorb the venom. Once the venom is adsorbed, the body can begin to heal itself more effectively.

Over 45,000 kits have been sold with only a .001 return rate for ineffectiveness—in spite of a lifetime money back guarantee. The company is rated A+ by the BBB, and we have been members since 2004.

Chapter 5

Eradicating the Brown Recluse Spider

Is eradication really possible? Pest control companies will not guarantee it, and if you find one that does, they are probably lying to you.

There are several reasons why the brown recluse spider is so difficult to eradicate:

1. Unlike insects, spiders do not clean themselves. Thus they do not typically ingest residual traces of insecticide just by crawling across the floor.

2. Brown recluses, unlike other spiders, don't ingest insecticide that might be sprayed on a prey-catching web. This is because they do not spin webs to catch prey and rarely use their silk.

3. Female brown recluses often live inside walls, boxes, or other out of the way places where pest control companies do not spray.

4. Male brown recluses typically hide out during the day when pest control companies do their spraying.

5. Unlike most spiders, brown recluses prefer dead prey over living prey. For this reason, when pesticides kill insects it only makes their lives even easier because they don't have to kill anything to have a meal. Less energy is spent and they can go longer in between meals as well.

   In fact, brown recluse spiders can eat an insect killed by insecticide just 24 hours prior. They will even feed on insects that have been dead for up to two months!

6. Research conducted at Oklahoma State and Texas A&M Universities confirm that brown recluse spiders are tenacious and are not killed by most insecticides, unless sprayed directly on the spider. However, even a spray of water can kill a brown recluse.

7. When pesticides are used, the more mobile male brown recluses simply flee the house en masse, as has been proven by researchers at Kansas University who set pitfall traps outside entry/exit points of homes that were being treated. Probably others were going to their favorite hiding place if they weren't hiding there already.

8. House spiders that are tremendously beneficial in the battle against brown recluse spiders can be killed by the pesticide, eliminating both competition for insects and potential enemies.

So the bottom line is you cannot necessarily completely eradicate the spider with 100 percent certainty. The only thing you can do is hope to contain them... especially in areas where they are indigenous.

Brown recluses live both inside and outside of the home. If you were to eliminate them all in one day, there could be more who are outside who find their way in.

Nevertheless, Kansas University researchers do make the statement that "effective population management is possible" with glue traps.

If you combine glue traps along with some other measures I will be describing later, eradication will be a possibility over a period of time. It won't be easy, but possible.

First, however, let's take a closer look as to why glue traps are so effective.

First of all, male brown recluses are very mobile and roam around every night looking for a meal. Unlike web-spinning spiders, they don't just sit and wait for an insect to inadvertently run or fly into their web. Instead, they go hunting. For this reason, setting traps is the ultimate alternative to spraying chemicals. Knowing their roaming habits will help even more.

Advantages of setting traps include:

1. You can determine whether or not your home actually has a brown recluse infestation.

2. Traps offer the opportunity to positively identify a brown recluse spider because it is caught on the trap. Your personal safety and the safety of your family are enhanced when you learn to recognize a brown recluse when you see one.

3. Traps can be placed in areas where it is not safe to spray pesticides, such as inside food cabinets.

4. They are inexpensive to use and do not require visits from an exterminator.

5. They are simple to use. Just fold your traps, set them in key locations, and you're done.

6. They enable you to identify which areas of your home are most infested by the brown recluse.

7. Other unwanted insects, such as cockroaches and crickets, will also get caught on the trap.

So where are the "key locations" to set the spider traps?

The diagram on the following page will illustrate the best places to put traps:

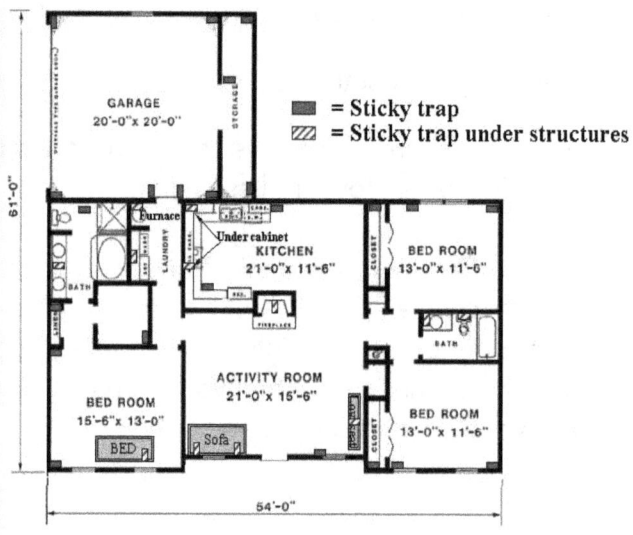

The above diagram is an illustration from Kansas University research, which has determined the top ten places to put spider traps:

Garage

One trap in each of the four corners is usually very effective. If you have an attached garage, place one trap on each side of the entrance to your home. If your garage has a storage room, place one trap on each corner and one near the doorway.

Bathroom

Behind the toilet.

Behind or along the side of the sink area.

Behind or underneath the bathtub, if possible. If not, a placement nearest the bathtub with help avoid spiders from entering the bathtub.

Bedrooms

Underneath the bed. This is one of the most important locations in your home because many spider bites occur while sleeping.

Along the outside wall near a window is the best location, but if this is not possible place them in a corner along an outside wall.

In closets, preferably along an outside wall.

Unused bedrooms are also important because spiders prefer undisturbed locations.

Kitchens

Underneath cabinets. Upper cabinet placement is generally ineffective.

In corners along the cabinet area (on the floor).

On the floor of a pantry closet.

Family/Living room

On window sills.

Near live plants, which draw insects.

Along the outside wall near a window is the best location, but if this is not possible place them in a corner along an outside wall.

Behind entertainment centers or bookshelves.

Basements

In piles of wood.

In boxes, especially clothing boxes.

Infrequently used areas and carpeted rooms.

Areas that were shown to NOT produce brown recluses, even in the most severe infestations, were:

1) Closet shelves

2) Inside upper kitchen cabinets

3) Inside drawers of desks and cabinets

4) Crawl spaces under houses

So how many glue traps should the average sized home contain? The above diagram shows a home that has 31 traps set. The average for a three-bedroom home with a garage is about 30 spider traps. If you have a larger home with a basement, more traps should be set.

The bottom line is this: The more traps you set, the more likely a spider is going to get caught in the trap. The more you set, the faster you will catch and help eliminate the spiders. The more spiders you eliminate, the less chance there will be for someone in your home to be bitten by one. It's simple math.

So what kind of glue trap should you purchase? This is an important question because not all glue traps are the same. Some glue traps have "gooey" glue that is soft and pliable. Other kinds have "sticky" glue. Some glue traps have a raised bed with the glue set down in the trap, while other kinds have a thin layer of glue over a flat surface.

Which type is best for catching brown recluses? This is an important question. You must buy the kinds that are sticky, and do not have a raised bed.

Why? Brown recluse spider behavior is such that they have a tendency to walk along walls. They will walk along the wall of one room until they run into a corner. Then, they will walk along the next wall, in search of prey.

If you set a trap out that has a raised bed, such as the one depicted below, the spider will think he has run into the corner of a wall and go around it. So the raised bed actually is a barrier to spider entrance.

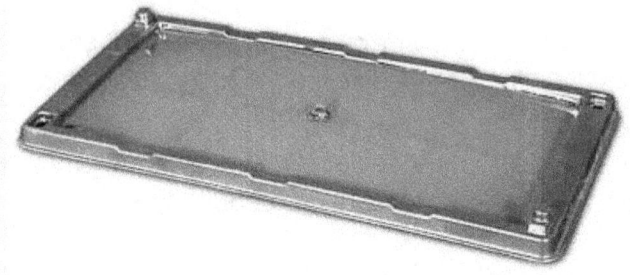

Traps with raised beds are most guilty for containing the "gooey glue," which does a poor job of catching brown recluses. Such traps are better suited for catching rodents or snakes.

So what kinds of traps contain the flat surface and "sticky" glue that is most effective for catching brown recluses?

When doing our research for the best traps available, we came across the Recluse Community Project headed by Kansas University. The team of researchers worked with the community in trapping or collecting some 86,000 brown recluse spiders for research. Through experience, they learned that the most effective trap available was the Catchmaster 288I.

For this reason, when we began offering our Brown Recluse First Aid Kit to the general public, we went with the Catchmaster 288I glue trap as an optional purchase. Each trap is small, but you can purchase quantities of 15 for about $0.67 per trap.

What other tactics can be used to help eradicate the spider? The next most important element would be reducing or eliminating potential entry and exit points for spiders and other insects in your home.

Install screens or replace damaged screens on doors and windows. Caulk or seal any cracks and crevices, even small ones. You would be amazed at how the brown recluse can scrunch down and squeeze into small cracks and openings. Chimneys, window sills, pipes, utility access holes and door thresholds are potential openings.

By sealing off entry and exit points, you are not only preventing the brown recluse spider from entering, you are also preventing its prey from having easy access as well. The spider isn't in your home to bite humans; it's in your home because there is food inside.

Understanding this, some misinformed pest control companies tell their customer's that they can help eliminate brown recluses by "getting rid of their prey." But as the head researcher of the Recluse Community Project stated, "There is no possible way to get rid of this spider's prey. Any organism that is able to survive on live prey, scavenge for dead prey, eat old dead prey or prey killed with insecticides, and will cannibalize its own on hard times, cannot be controlled by eliminating its prey."

Add in the factor that this spider is able to live for six months without food and water, and you have a spider that cannot be eradicated by prey elimination alone!

The next most important tactic for eliminating brown recluse populations is sealing off potential hiding places.

Outside the home you can remove potential breeding grounds like wood piles, leaf litter, debris and rocks that may be close to your home.

Inside the home you can seal up boxes and storage bags. Also, keep any unsealed hiding place away from the wall if possible. Reducing the amount of undisturbed clutter in your home will help reduce the number of brown recluse hiding places. With gloves on, you can inspect clothing that is infrequently worn and store it in sealed boxes and bags when not in use.

You can also help prevent them from being able to easily breed in your walls by caulking the baseboards, door molding, and other openings in the ceilings and walls created by light fixtures, electrical outlets and light switches.

Brown recluses are experts at hiding, thus the name "recluse." To be sure that you don't miss any openings, take a flashlight and look for brown recluse spiders roaming around your house at night. If you see one, they will usually not be too far from where they chose to hide. When you find one, kill it with a broom or shoe and see if you can discover its hiding place. If you find it, seal it up.

Also, engaging in routine house cleaning with a vacuum along walls and crevices will help eliminate spider egg sacs, spiders and webs.

However, normal house spiders like the cobweb weaving variety commonly seen in homes are actually major predators of the brown recluse. For this reason, you might choose to leave their egg sacs alone. They are harmless to humans but often quite deadly to brown recluses.

Cobweb weaving spiders (*A. tepidariorum* and *S. triangulosa*) often seen in homes are the main predators of the brown recluse.

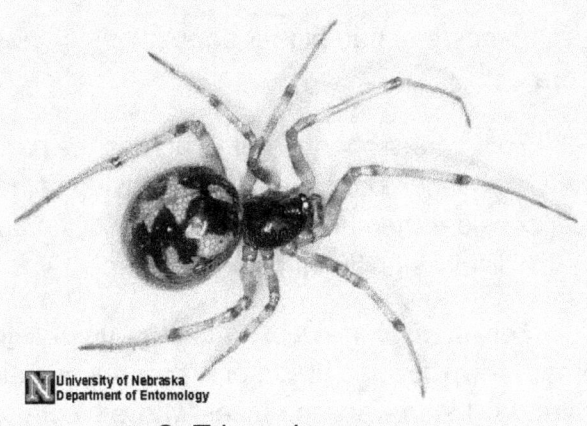

S. Triangulosa

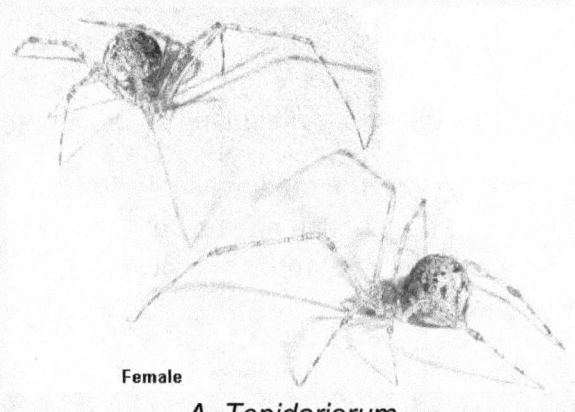

Female

A. Tepidariorum

These spiders have veracious appetites and can eat several brown recluses a day. They are experts at handling prey larger than they are and have very effective venom for killing brown recluses.

Home studies have proven that there is definitely a clear relationship between the populations of cobweb weaving spiders and brown recluses.

Of homes that did have a brown recluse spider infestation, the populations of brown recluses were much less in homes that had higher populations of these other spiders.

So if you happen to come across the harmless, but somewhat scarier looking cobweb weaving spiders in your home, consider them to be a natural pesticide against the more medically significant brown recluse!

This same correlation was not true of cellar spiders, another brown recluse predator. This was because cellar spiders don't spin webs in places where brown recluses typically roam.

Brown recluse spiders can be found in both old and new homes. Field studies showed that newer homes were just as likely to have an infestation as older homes.

A survey of 100 randomly selected homes demonstrated that "house age has absolutely nothing to do with the presence, or number of brown recluse spiders found in the house."

A number of homes less than a year old had immense brown recluse problems. How could this be?

There are several possible reasons:

1) New homes often encroach on existing brown recluse territory. Perhaps no other spider has adapted so well and benefited so much from human encroachment into their former habitat.

2) Construction materials packed in crates and boxes often bring brown recluses with them.

3) While the home is being built, it is more open to insects and spiders entering and exiting freely.

4) Brown recluses will often hitch a ride in boxes and furniture brought from the homeowner's former location.

If you currently have an infestation, how can you avoid bringing brown recluse spiders with you when moving to a new location? This is a concern for many.

Here are some tips to help you avoid packing the brown recluse spider along with all of your other belongings:

- USE LONG GLOVES WHEN PACKING. Brown recluses cannot bite through gloves or clothing.

- Use plastic tubs, bins, bags or crates rather than cardboard boxes when moving. Brown recluses cannot easily negotiate smooth surfaces such as porcelain and plastic. With totes, if one does happen to ride along with you, you will more than likely notice it because it will be permanently trapped in the tub or crate and unable to escape.

- If you decide to use cardboard boxes, thoroughly tape each flap and seam with strong, sticky tape to prevent a brown recluse from being able to slip into the box. Brown recluses have very flat bodies that can slip into the smallest of crevices. Leave no hole or flap unsealed.

- Shake out each item of clothing that you bring to ensure that they are not hiding out in your shirts, pants, coats and other cloth garments. Remember, brown recluses have little pinchers at the ends of their feet for holding on to things. For this reason you will have to shake the clothing vigorously for them to come out. Also shake out papers and other objects that may be a hiding place for brown recluses.

- Thoroughly inspect and vacuum your furniture just before loading it onto the moving truck—especially underneath. Be careful, though, with vacuuming, which has been known to agitate the spiders and increases the chances of being bitten.

- Do not pack late at night. This is the worst time to pack because it is when the spiders are most active and able to climb into the things you are packing. Packing is such a busy time that you may not notice.

- Place spider traps near the boxes to catch them, and if you are not through with packing a box, seal it off with tape each night anyway to prevent a wandering brown recluse from entering it in search for food or a mate.

Another line of defense is "awareness." While you are working on eradicating the brown recluse spider from your home, you need to be aware of the ways in which other people have been bitten by the spider. They are:

1. Rolling over them on the bed at night.

2. Most victims are actually bitten while sleeping. By having "dust ruffles" along the edge of your bed, you are providing a way for the spider to climb up onto your bed and, out of a desire to not get crushed, bite you while you are sleeping and happen to roll over them. If you have dust ruffles, make sure they are not near the floor.

3. Place glue traps underneath your bed to catch any spiders that may come near it.

4. Remember that brown recluses cannot easily negotiate smooth surfaces. This means they are unlikely to climb up the smooth surfaced feet that your bed frame may rest on.

5. If you have a ceiling fixture in your bedroom, seal it off from the attic or second floor. Brown recluses are notorious for dropping down off the ceilings and onto the floor or your bed at night.

6. When putting on clothing or shoes.

7. Always inspect and shake out your clothing when putting it on. Brown recluses can hide in dresser drawers and closets, but the most common way of getting bitten is from clothing lying around the floor or on furniture. A woman in St. Louis died because she did not know to follow this

step.

8. Shake out your shoes before putting them on. Brown recluse fangs cannot penetrate the soles of your feet or even the palms of your hands, but they can bite any other areas of your foot as you crush them while putting on your shoes.

9. When taking a bath or shower.

   Always inspect the tub or shower before you turn on the faucet. If you have a significant infestation, brown recluses can be found there several times a year. This is because they are trapped within the smooth surfaces of the tub. Again, they do not have sticky feet but have pinchers which cannot negotiate smooth surfaces.

   Remember the woman who was bitten by the recluse spider while taking a shower? She found the spider on her foot, and due to complications arising from the bite wound, the leg had to be amputated. An infection had reached the bone and there was nothing else they could do. Her foot no longer exists!

10. When cleaning, organizing, or getting into areas that are typically undisturbed.

    Wearing long gloves will help to eliminate unintentional contact with the brown recluse spider in these areas. If you find the spider, also look for an egg sac nearby. If you see one, remove it and flush it down the toilet.

If you are among those who are fascinated by these spiders and want to study them or observe them more closely, there is a fairly easy way of catching them.

One thing to remember is that these spiders go from zero to blurring fast in .00001 seconds. They have eight legs that will propel them along very quickly so they can be tricky to capture, especially if they are males.

To capture these spiders, take the following steps:

1) Obtain a wide mouth jar (plastic jars and containers are best) and place it in an easily accessible area.

2) Along with the jar, keep a piece of light poster board, card stock, or plastic long enough and wide enough to cover the mouth of the jar.

3) Upon discovering a recluse, take the jar and slowly cover the spider without touching any part of its body.

4) Next, slide the poster board, card stock, or plastic under the jar to enclose the spider in the jar.

5) Carefully turn the jar over so that the spider falls into the bottom of the jar.

6) Put the lid on the jar. Don't worry about making "breathing holes."

Once the spider is in the jar, it is unlikely that he will be able to climb out even if the lid is not on because, again, they cannot negotiate smooth surfaces.

There is also a myth floating around that using a dehumidifier will reduce brown recluse populations. The premise is that spiderling and juvenile brown recluses need sufficient moisture in the air to survive. But this could hardly be any farther from the truth. Brown recluses are built to endure harsh, dry, hot, desert type environments.

Research actually indicates that high humidity will kill brown recluse spiders. Spiderlings in particular have a high death toll in high humidity. Dehumidifiers will actually help create a more favorable environment for brown recluses!

Chapter 6

Identifying a Recluse Spider

Identifying a recluse spider doesn't have to be difficult. Experts will often say that we need their help because in most cases we do. But with the information I am providing in this chapter, the average person will be able to easily identify whether or not a particular spider is a recluse species.

The spider you identify as a recluse species will most likely be a brown recluse if you happen to live in its indigenous area. It may be one of the desert varieties if you live in Texas, California or the desert southwest.

One thing that you need to remember when it comes to identifying recluses is that THEY MUST look a certain way in order to be a genuine recluse. Don't let fear lead you to believe that just because it looks similar, it might still be a recluse spider.

So let's start by learning what a recluse spider CANNOT have, so that you can at least eliminate a high percentage of the more than 20,000 spider species found in the United States.

What recluses do NOT look like:

1. Recluse spiders do NOT have stripes or markings on their abdomen or belly. They also never have a pointed end. They are ALWAYS rounded and a solid color, as shown below:

Fuller, Lighter Brown Abdomen   Smaller, Dark Brown Abdomen

2. Recluse spiders do NOT have stripes or markings on their legs. Brown recluse legs are ALWAYS a fairly solid color, as shown below:

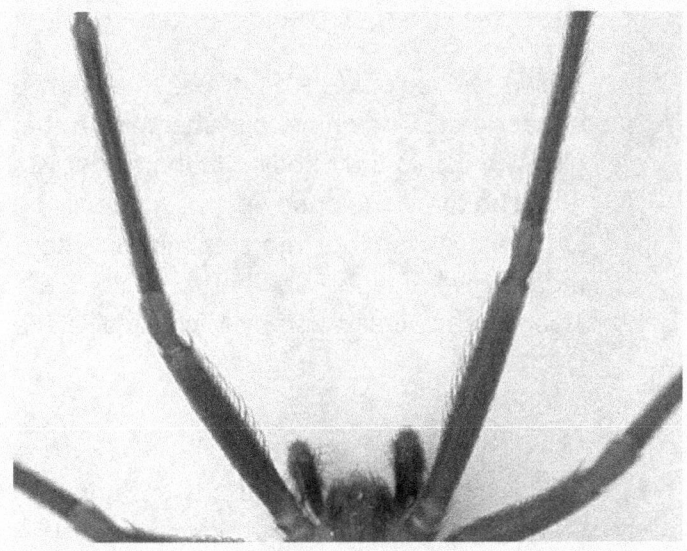

3. Brown recluses do not look "fuzzy" or "hairy" unless you have extremely good eyesight or a high resolution camera like the above photo. They also don't look particularly intimidating. See below

photo:

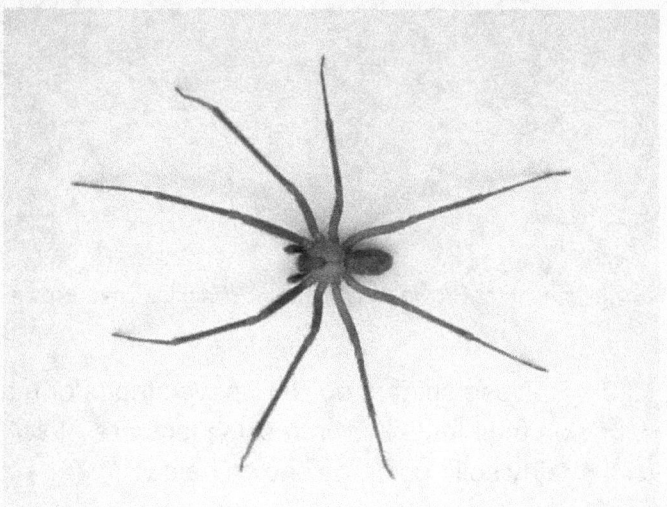

4. Brown recluse spiders do not have a shiny or waxy
   appearance. They have a matte finish rather than a
   glossy finish to their bodies. If the spider is shiny, it
   might be the woodlouse spider, which also happens
   to have six eyes (not in a semi-circle pattern) and is
   more active at night. See below photo of a
   woodlouse spider taken by Michel Vuijlsteke:

NOT A BROWN RECLUSE

5. A brown recluse spider does not have a conspicuous web. Irregular webbing might be seen in a nesting area, but it is not for catching prey. The below photo is a brown recluse nesting area with a juvenile spider nearby:

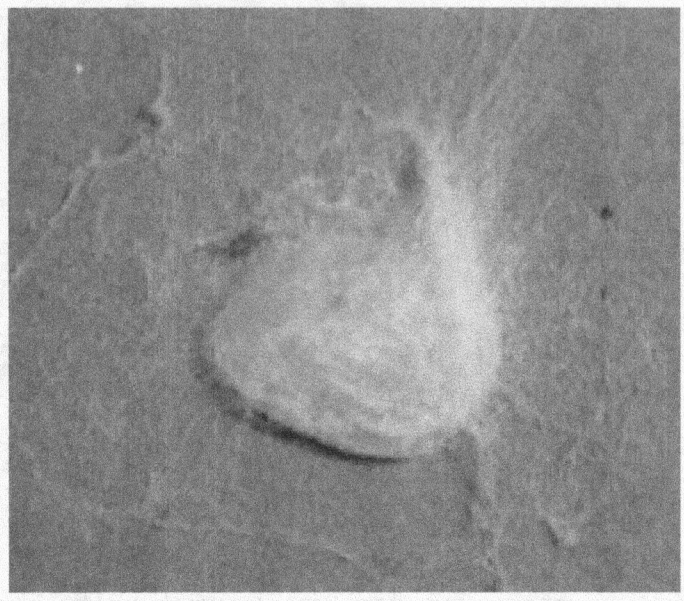

6. The BODY portion of a brown recluse (not including the legs) has never been seen to be larger than a half-inch. If it is a large-bodied spider, it cannot be a brown recluse. See below photo for an example of two different sized brown recluse spiders:

Now that you have six tips on what a recluse spider is NOT, let's focus on what the brown recluse actually is.

The Violin Marking

Along with the color, the violin pattern might be the most distinguishing characteristic of the brown recluse spider and some of the other recluse species. However, there are other spiders which might also appear to have a pattern on their back similar to a violin.

For this reason, recognition of the violin pattern along with the above tips on what a brown recluse spider is NOT, will serve to help positively identify your species.

Here is the violin pattern on the infamous brown recluse:

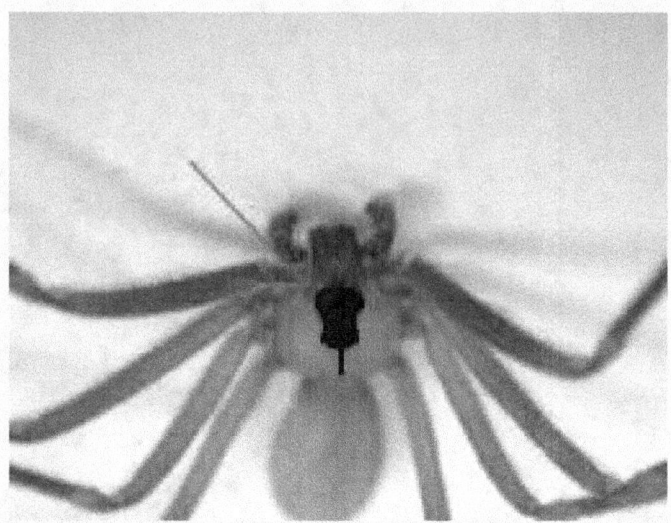

The above photo, again, is edited to help you identify the location of the violin pattern. Here is the same photo, unedited:

Below are four other photos of the brown recluse, with a focus on the violin pattern on its back:

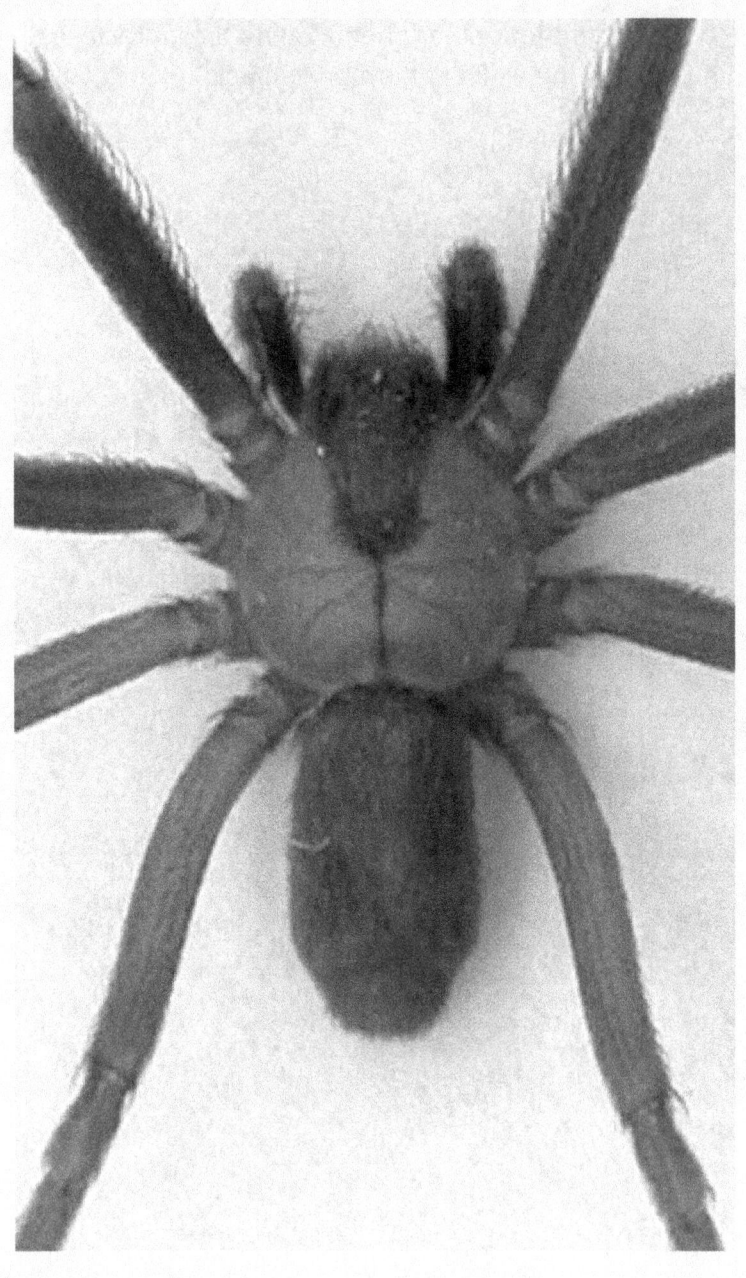

Here are some spiders that look like brown
recluses but have other character qualities that eliminate
them from being a recluse species:

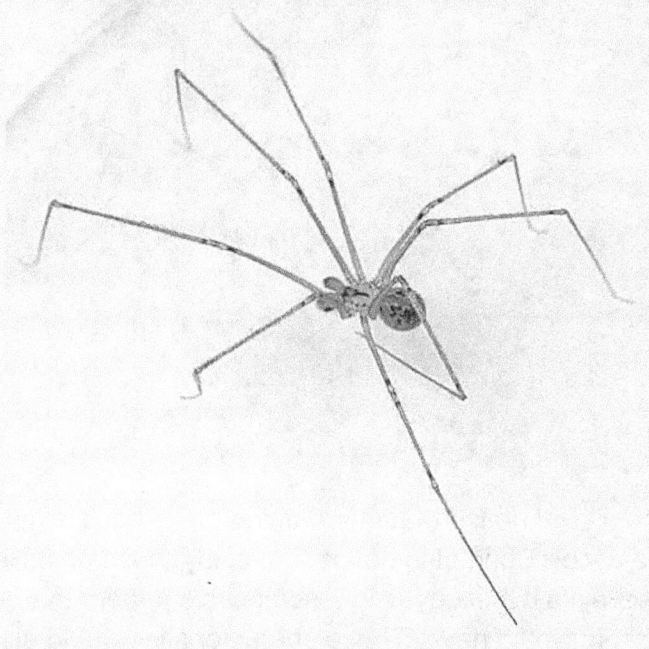

The spider might, at first glance, appear to have the violin marking on its back, but notice that this spider, a type of cellar spider under the *Psilochorus* genus, has markings on the legs and on the abdomen.

Also notice the longer, thinner legs in proportion to the spider's body. Furthermore, these spiders spin webs to catch prey, whereas brown recluses do not. These characteristics eliminate the spider from being a recluse species.

Another brown recluse look-a-like is the kukulcania, or southern house spider:

But notice that the marking on its back is not quite like a violin, and also notice the "spiny" hairs on its legs. It also lacks the six eyes in a semi-circle pattern that a brown recluse would have. These characteristics would eliminate the spider from being a recluse species.

The Eyes Have It

If you are able to acquire a magnifying glass, the brown recluse spider has six eyes arranged in a triangular pattern of three sets.

The sets are called dyads, and if you can see them clearly at the bell end of the violin marking, this is clear proof that the spider is a recluse species. See the below photo:

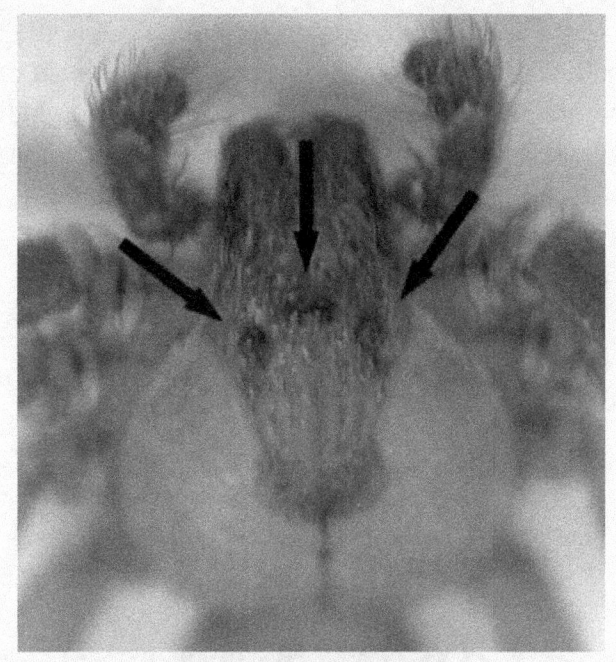

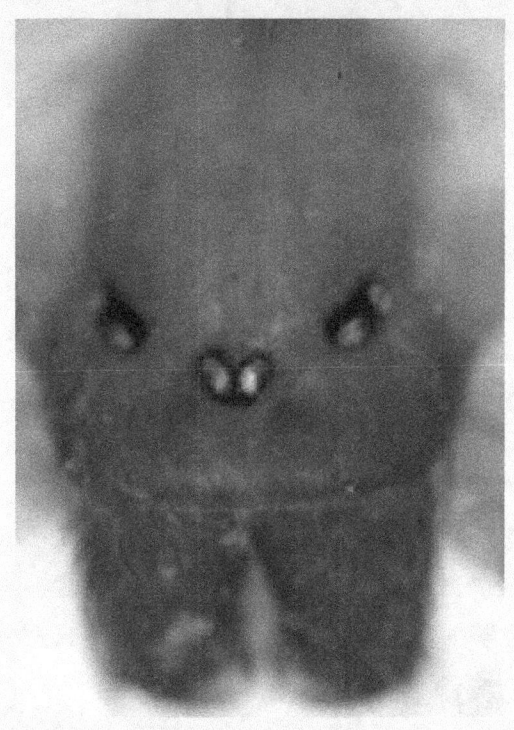

The eye pattern alone is not sufficient to determine whether or not the spider is a recluse species. For instance, the *Scytodes* or spitting spider shares this pattern as well. But the *Scytodes* has markings all over its body and looks nothing like a recluse:

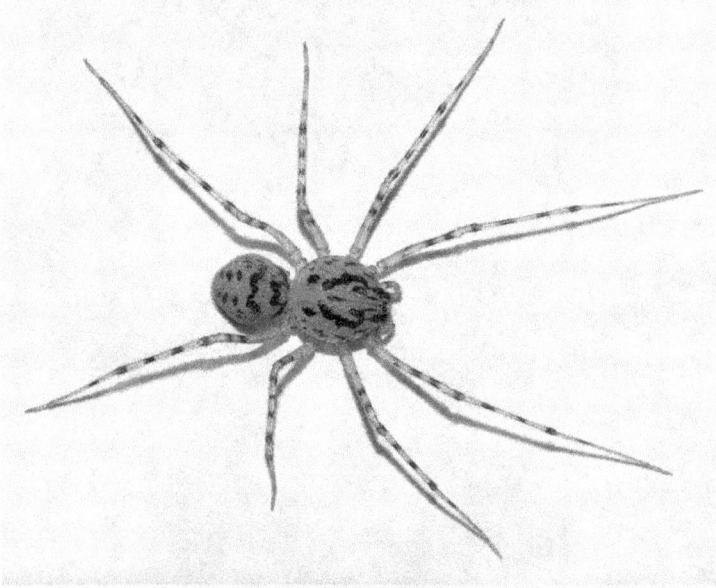

So now that you have this important information, you are now equipped to positively identify a recluse species of spider. Now you can be the person that others look to when the question is asked, "Could this be a recluse?"

Chapter 7

Summary

Chapter 7 – Summary

The brown recluse and other recluse species of spiders are among the most fascinating spiders to study and learn about. They are also one of the most misunderstood.

Brown recluse bites are also notoriously difficult to identify, with much of the medical community diagnosing a person with a brown recluse bite when in reality they have an infection or some other skin condition.

In short, the brown recluse spider is shrouded in controversy and much confusion. Only those who are informed can sort through the controversy, confusion and misinformation. Resolving this dilemma has been part of my goal in producing this book.

Another goal I have is that others will know how to avoid getting bitten by the brown recluse spider, and perhaps save my fellow man from experiencing the excruciating pain that such a bite can put a person through, not to mention the potential of losing one's life or limb.

Even if a person does not lose their life, which is certainly rare, the medical bills and loss of time at work can be a very difficult and challenging experience.

In the midst of the confusion, however, one thing is very clear. Brown recluse spiders are here to stay. And since they thrive when human populations take over uninhabited land, they will continue to benefit from their relationships with us.

We might as well learn about them and how to respond to them because whether we like it or not, they want to live in our homes with us.

It is true that many people live with hundreds of brown recluses in their homes and yet never get bitten by the spider.

They would rather that we don't even know they are here with us. They would prefer to avoid us completely, and they have no desire or intent to inflict harm on us.

But if we happen to cross paths, there is a chance that our encounter might change our lives forever.